# HSP Math

## UNIT 6

Harcourt
SCHOOL PUBLISHERS

Visit *The Learning Site!*
www.harcourtschool.com

Part Number  9997-85171-4

8 9 10 11 12   1678   15 14 13 12 11
4500332399

## Senior Authors

**Evan M. Maletsky**
Professor Emeritus
Montclair State University
Upper Montclair, New Jersey

**Joyce McLeod**
Visiting Professor, Retired
Rollins College
Winter Park, Florida

## Authors

**Karen S. Norwood**
Associate Professor of
   Mathematics Education
North Carolina State University
Raleigh, North Carolina

**Tom Roby**
Associate Professor
   of Mathematics
Director, Quantitative
   Learning Center
University of Connecticut
Storrs, Connecticut

**James A. Mendoza Epperson**
Associate Professor
Department of Mathematics
The University of Texas
   at Arlington
Arlington, Texas

**Juli K. Dixon**
Associate Professor of
   Mathematics Education
University of Central Florida
Orlando, Florida

**Janet K. Scheer**
Executive Director
Create-A-Vision
Foster City, California

**David G. Wright**
Professor
Department of Mathematics
Brigham Young University
Provo, Utah

**David D. Molina**
Program Director, Retired
The Charles A. Dana Center
The University of Texas
   at Austin

**Jennie M. Bennett**
Mathematics Teacher
Houston Independent
   School District
Houston, Texas

**Lynda Luckie**
Director, K–12 Mathematics
Gwinnett County Public Schools
Suwanee, Georgia

**Angela G. Andrews**
Assistant Professor of
   Math Education
National Louis University
Lisle, Illinois

**Vicki Newman**
Classroom Teacher
McGaugh Elementary School
Los Alamitos Unified
   School District
Seal Beach, California

**Barbara Montalto**
Mathematics Consultant
Assistant Director of
   Mathematics, Retired
Texas Education Agency
Austin, Texas

**Minerva Cordero-Epperson**
Associate Professor of Mathematics
   and Associate Dean of the
   Honors College
The University of Texas
   at Arlington
Arlington, Texas

## Program Consultants and Specialists

**Russell Gersten**
Director, Instructional
   Research Group
Long Beach, California
Professor Emeritus of
   Special Education
University of Oregon
Eugene, Oregon

**Michael DiSpezio**
Writer and On-Air Host,
   JASON Project
North Falmouth,
   Massachusetts

**Concepcion Molina**
Southwest Educational
   Development Lab
Austin, Texas

**Rebecca Valbuena**
Language Development
   Specialist
Stanton Elementary School
Glendora, California

**Valerie Johse**
Elementary Math Specialist
Office of Curriculum
   & Instruction
Pearland I.S.D.
Pearland, Texas

**Robin C. Scarcella**
Professor and Director,
   Program of Academic
   English and ESL
University of California, Irvine
Irvine, California

**Lydia Song**
Mathematics Program
   Specialist
Costa Mesa, California

**Tyrone Howard**
Assistant Professor,
   UCLA Graduate School
   of Education—
   Information Studies
University of California
   at Los Angeles
Los Angeles, California

**Anne M. Goodrow**
Associate Professor,
   Elementary Education
Rhode Island College
Providence, Rhode Island

# The Great Outdoors

written by Margie Sigman

In this story you will also **TALK Math** and **WRITE Math**.

**Family Note:** This story will help your child review one more and one fewer.

A

I big sand castle

By the edge of the sea.

If I place I more rock,

How many will there be?

Science

What do you see at the beach?

2 shells on my castle

By the edge of the sea.

If I place 1 more shell,

How many will there be?

_____

Science

What floats on the ocean?

C

3 cups on my castle

By the edge of the sea,

If I place 1 more cup,

How many will there be?

_____
_ _ _ _
_____

Science

How does ocean water taste?

4 flags on my castle

By the edge of the sea.

If I place 1 more flag,

How many will there be?

_____
_ _ _ _ _
_____

Science

I fine sand castle

By the edge of the sea.

When the waves come rolling in,

How many will there be?

Science

What do waves do?

## My Math Story
### Literature Activity

**Vocabulary Review**

one more

one fewer

**DIRECTIONS** Draw a sand castle. Draw 8 objects on the sand castle. Share a story about your sandcastle with a classmate.

**G**

# One More and One Fewer

**DIRECTIONS 1.** Draw a set with one more shell.
**2.** Draw a set with one fewer shell.

H

# School Home CONNECTION

## Dear Family,

My class started Unit 6 today. I will learn about addition and subtraction. Here are some vocabulary words and activities for us to share.

Love, _____

## Vocabulary Power

### Key Math Vocabulary

**Add** to combine; to join two separate sets and find the total quantity

**Subtract** the process of finding out how many are left when a number of items are taken away from a set

### Vocabulary Activity

**Math on the Move**

Show your child a set of 5 objects and a set of 2 objects. Ask him or her how many objects in all.

**GO ONLINE**

**Technology**
Multimedia Math Gloassary link at
**www.harcourtschool.com/hspmath**

© Harcourt

# School Home CONNECTION

## Remember This

Your child may already know how to tell you how many objects there will be if you add one more to a set.

## Calendar Activity

### March

| Sunday | Monday | Tuesday | Wednesday | Thursday | Friday | Saturday |
|--------|--------|---------|-----------|----------|--------|----------|
| 1 | 2 | 3 | 4 | 5 | 6 | 7 |
| 8 | 9 | 10 | 11 | 12 | 13 | 14 |
| 15 | 16 | 17 | 18 | 19 | 20 | 21 |
| 22 | 23 | 24 | 25 | 26 | 27 | 28 |
| 29 | 30 | 31 | | | | |

Ask your child to add all the Wednesdays and all the Saturdays in this month.

**Practice** (after pages 301 and 302)

Have your child use red to circle the days in one week he or she goes to school. Now have him or her use blue to circle the days in one week he or she does not go to school. Write an addition sentence to show this.

**Practice** (after pages 327 and 328)

Have your child color all the days in one week. Now have your child mark an x on the days in one week that he or she does not go to school. Write a subtraction sentence to show this.

## Literature

Look for these books in a library. Ask your child to point out math vocabulary words as you read each book together.

**Toy Box Subtraction.**
Fuller, Jill.
Children's Press, 2005.

**Addition Annie.**
Gisler, David.
Children's Press, 2002.

**Construction Countdown.**
Olson, K. C.
Henry Holt, 2004.

© Harcourt

## Show What You Know

 **1**

 **2**

**DIRECTIONS** 1-2. Circle the set that has more.

 **Family Note:** This page checks your child's understanding of important concepts and skills needed for success in Chapter 11.

# Problem Solving Workshop
## Strategy • Act It Out

**DIRECTIONS** 1-2. Listen to and act out the story. Write the number that shows how many children in all.

**OBJECTIVE** • Solve problems by using the strategy *act it out.*

 **HOME ACTIVITY** • Tell your child a short story about adding 2 objects to a group of 5. Have your child use toys to act out the story and then write the number that shows how many objects in all.

**294** two hundred ninety-four

© Harcourt

 **1**

**3**

**1**

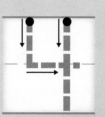

**2**

**2**

**4**

**3**

**8**

**2**

**DIRECTIONS** 1–3. Listen to the story. Model the story with cubes. Draw the cubes. Write the number that shows how many in all.

OBJECTIVE • Use concrete objects to model addition.

**1**

3     3    

**2**

2     6

**3**

4     5

**DIRECTIONS** 1–3. Listen to the story. Model the story with cubes. Draw the cubes. Write the number that shows how many in all.

**HOME ACTIVITY** • Tell your child a short vacation story about adding 3 objects to a group of 4. Have your child use small objects such as beans to make each group in the story and then write the number that shows how many objects in all.

**1**

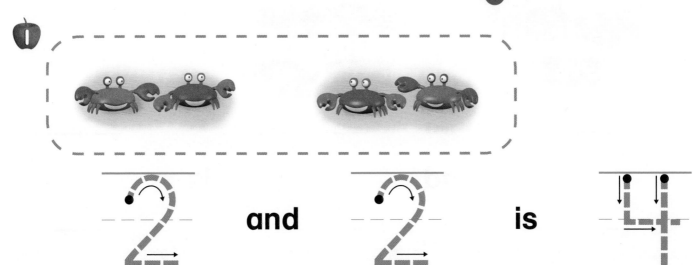

2 and 2 is 4

**2**

_____ and _____ is _____

**3**

_____ and _____ is _____

**DIRECTIONS** 1–3. Place cubes on the objects in each group. Write how many in each group. Circle the two groups. Write how many in all.

OBJECTIVE • Use objects and pictures to understand joining groups.

**1**

_____     _____     _____

___ **and** ___ **is** ___

**2**

_____     _____     _____

___ **and** ___ **is** ___

**3**

_____     _____     _____

___ **and** ___ **is** ___

**DIRECTIONS**   1–3. Write how many in each group. Circle the two groups. Write how many in all.

 **HOME ACTIVITY** · Have your child draw a group of 2 beach balls and a group of 7 beach balls. Have your child write how many beach balls are in each group. Then have him or her write how many beach balls in all.

**298**   two hundred ninety-eight

# Introduce Symbols to Add

**1**

**4** and **3** is **7**

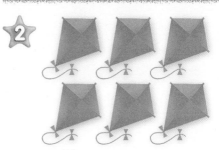 + 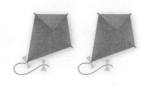 ===

**2**

**6** and **2** is **8**

_____  +  _____  ===  _____

**3**

**3** and **6** is **9**

_____  +  _____  ===  _____

**DIRECTIONS 1–3.** Write how many in each group. Circle the two groups. Trace the symbols. Write how many in all.

OBJECTIVE • Use symbols to represent addition sentences.

**1**

2 and 5 is 7

2 + 5 = 7

**2**

5 and 2 is 7

___ + ___ = ___

**3**

6 and 4 is 10

___ + ___ = ___

**DIRECTIONS** 1–3. Write how many in each group. Circle the two groups. Trace the symbols. Write how many in all.

 **HOME ACTIVITY** · Have your child use small objects to model one of the addition sentences on this page. Then have him or her combine the groups before the = to show the same amount as the number after the =.

**300** three hundred

© Harcourt

Name _____

 ## ✓ Mid Chapter 11 Review

 **1**

# 3          4

_____
- - - - -
_____

 **2**

          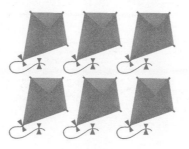

_____          _____          _____
- - - - - **and** - - - - - **is** - - - - -
_____          _____          _____

 **3**

          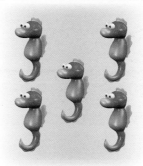

**2**    **and**    **6**    **is**    **8**

_____          _____          _____
- - - - -  ╬  - - - - -  ═  - - - - -

**DIRECTIONS** 1. Model the numbers with cubes. Draw the cubes. Write the number that shows how many in all. 2. Write how many in each group. Circle the two groups. Write how many in all. 3. Write how many in each group. Circle the two groups. Trace the symbols. Write how many in all.

 © Harcourt

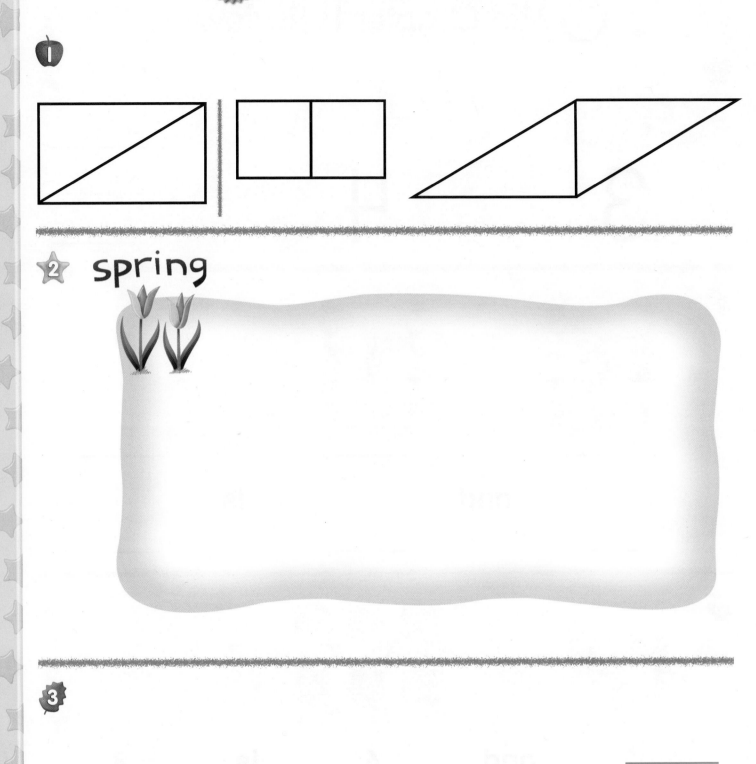

**①**

**②** spring

**③**

4     2     _____

**DIRECTIONS   1.** Find two plane figures that make the figure at the beginning of the row. Use these two figures to find the figure that has the same area as the figure at the beginning of the row. Circle the figure. **2.** Look at the name of the season. Draw something that happens in that season.   **3.** Model the numbers with cubes. Draw the cubes. Write the number that tells how many in all.

Name _____ **Addition Patterns**

 **1**

$$1 + 1 =$$

**2**

$$2 + 1 =$$ _____

**3**

$$3 + 1 =$$ _____

**4**

$$4 + 1 =$$ _____

**DIRECTIONS   1–4. How many shells? Draw one more shell. Write the number of shells in all to complete the addition sentence.**

OBJECTIVE • Represent an addition pattern of one more in addition sentences.

**Chapter 11 • Lesson 5**   three hundred three **303**

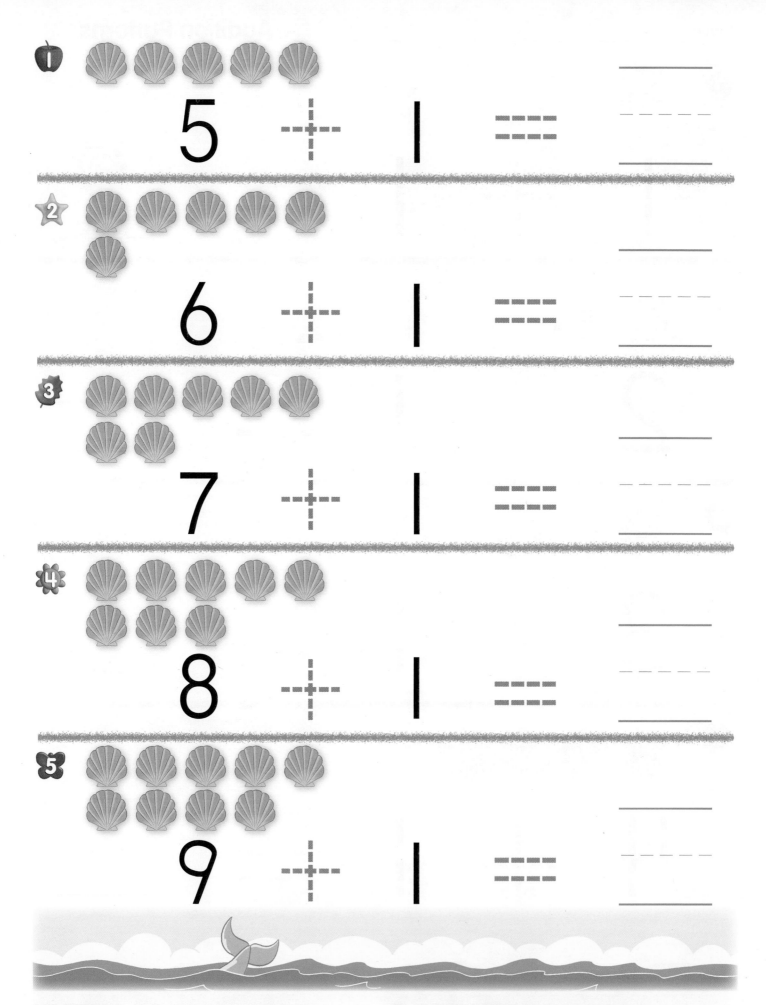

**1** $5 + 1 = $ _____

**2** $6 + 1 = $ _____

**3** $7 + 1 = $ _____

**4** $8 + 1 = $ _____

**5** $9 + 1 = $ _____

**DIRECTIONS** 1–5. How many shells? Draw one more shell. Write the number of shells in all to complete the addition sentence.

 **HOME ACTIVITY** • Draw objects in a column beginning with a set of 1 to a set of 9. Have your child draw one more object beside each set, and write how many in all.

© Harcourt

# Addition Sentences

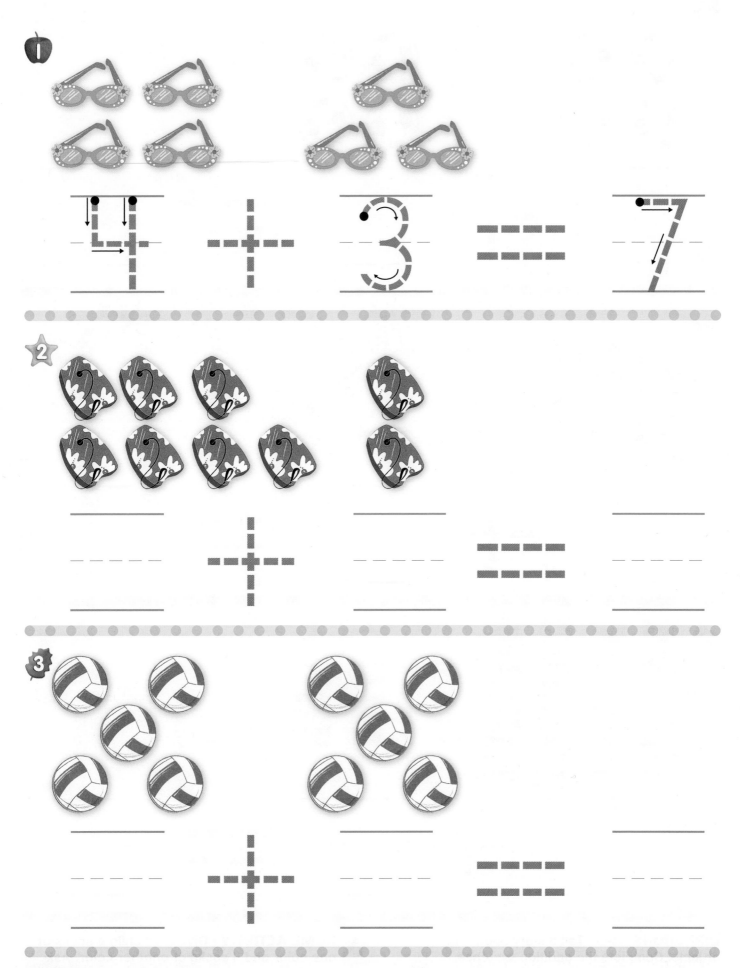

**1** $4 + 3 = 7$

**2** ___ + ___ = ___

**3** ___ + ___ = ___

**DIRECTIONS** Tell a story about the objects. Complete the addition sentence.

OBJECTIVE • Complete simple addition sentences.

**Chapter 11 • Lesson 6**

three hundred five **305**

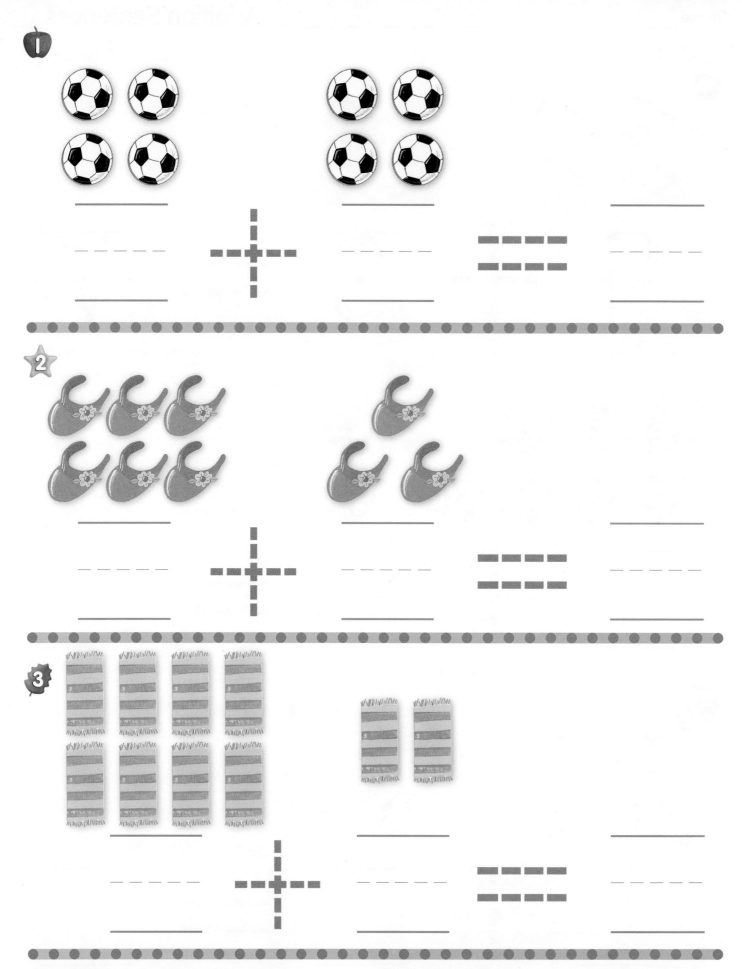

**1**

_____   +   _____   =   _____
_____       _____       _____

**2**

_____   +   _____   =   _____
_____       _____       _____

**3**

_____   +   _____   =   _____
_____       _____       _____

**DIRECTIONS** 1–3. Tell a story about the objects. Complete the addition sentence.

 **HOME ACTIVITY** · Give your child 6 socks of one color and 4 socks of another color. Ask your child to tell a story about the socks. Then write this addition sentence, and have your child complete it: _ + _ = _.

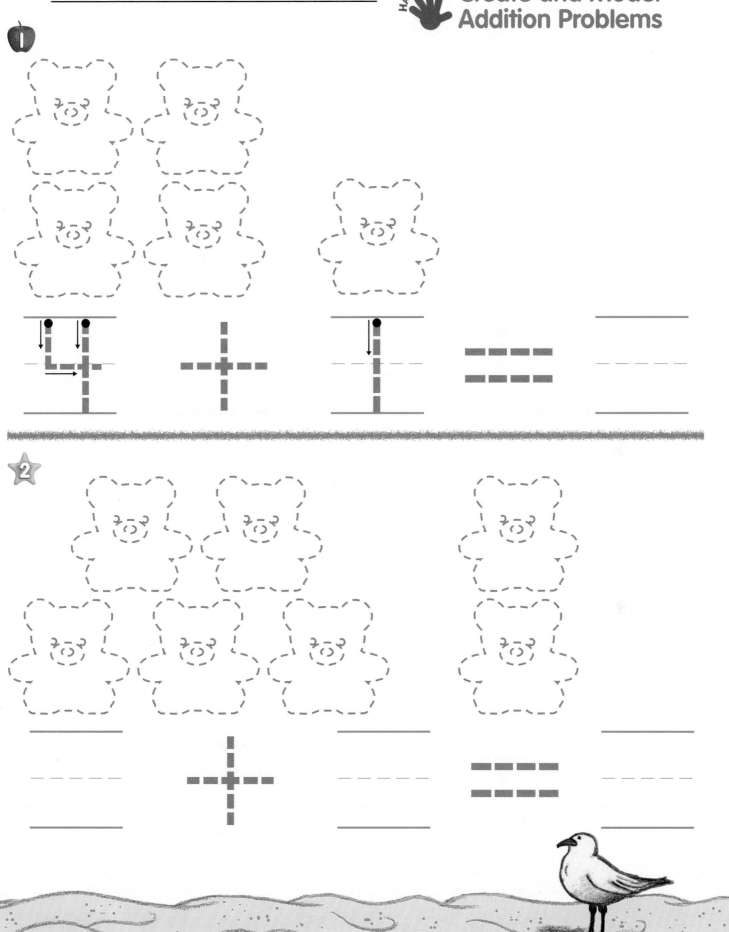

**DIRECTIONS**  1–2. Tell an addition story. Model your story with counters. Color the counters. Use count on to find the sum. Complete the addition sentence.

**OBJECTIVE** • Use concrete objects to create and model an addition problem.

**1**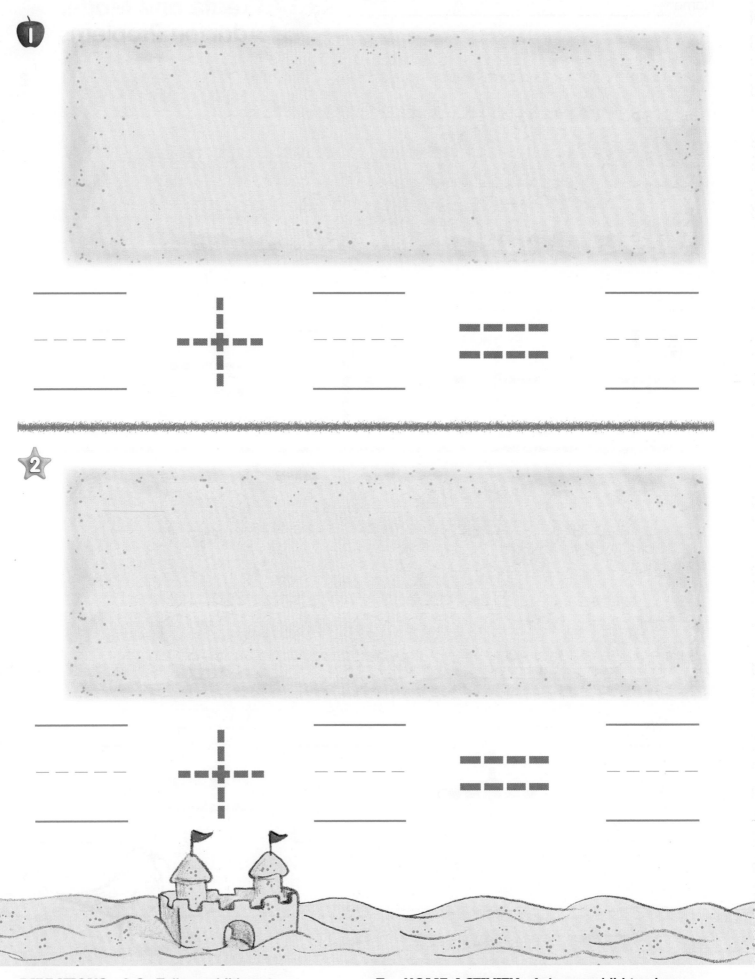

____  ____  $+$  ____  ____  $=$  ____  ____

_____

**2**

____  ____  $+$  ____  ____  $=$  ____  ____

**DIRECTIONS   1–2.** Tell an addition story. Model your story with counters. Draw the counters. Use count on to find the sum. Complete the addition sentence.

 **HOME ACTIVITY ·** Ask your child to choose one problem on the page. Have your child tell you the addition story and then explain how the addition sentence shows the story.

**308**  three hundred eight

**Use Pennies to Add**

**1**

$$4¢ \ + \ \underline{\quad}¢ \ = \ 6¢$$

**2**

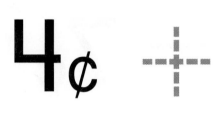

$$5¢ \ + \ \underline{\quad}¢ \ = \ 8¢$$

**DIRECTIONS** 1–2. Use pennies to find the missing number. Draw the pennies. Write the missing number.

OBJECTIVE • Use pennies to solve addition problems.

**1**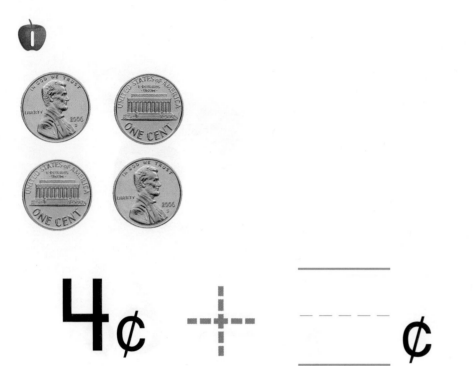

$$4¢ + \underline{\hspace{2cm}}¢ = 7¢$$

**2**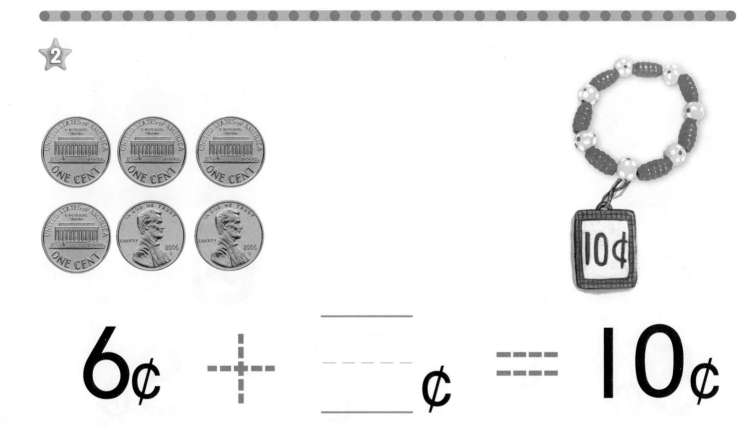

$$6¢ + \underline{\hspace{2cm}}¢ = 10¢$$

**DIRECTIONS** 1–2. Use pennies to find the missing number. Draw the pennies. Write the missing number.

 **HOME ACTIVITY** · Show your child an object with a price tag of up to 10 cents. Show your child a group of pennies less than the amount of the object. Ask your child to tell you how many more pennies they need to buy the object.

**1**

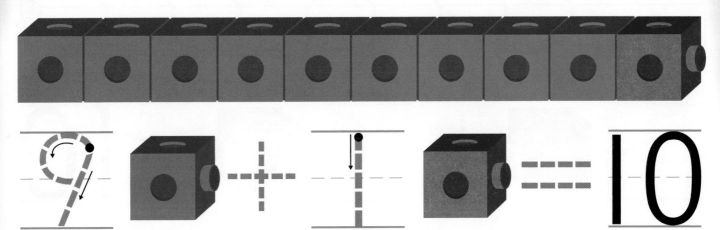

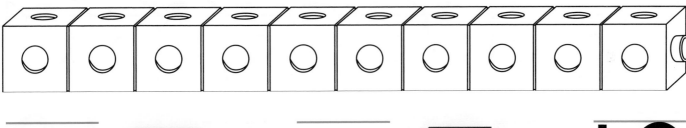

9     +    1     =    10

**2**

_____    +    _____    =    10

**3**

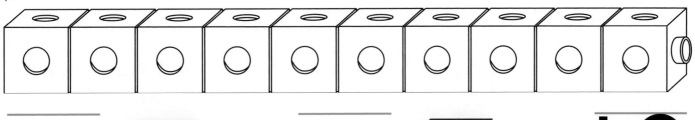

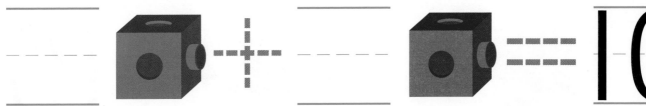

_____    +    _____    =    10

**DIRECTIONS** 1–3. Use two colors of cubes to show different ways to make 10. Color the cubes. Complete the addition sentence for each model.

OBJECTIVE • Solve problems by using the skill *use a model.*

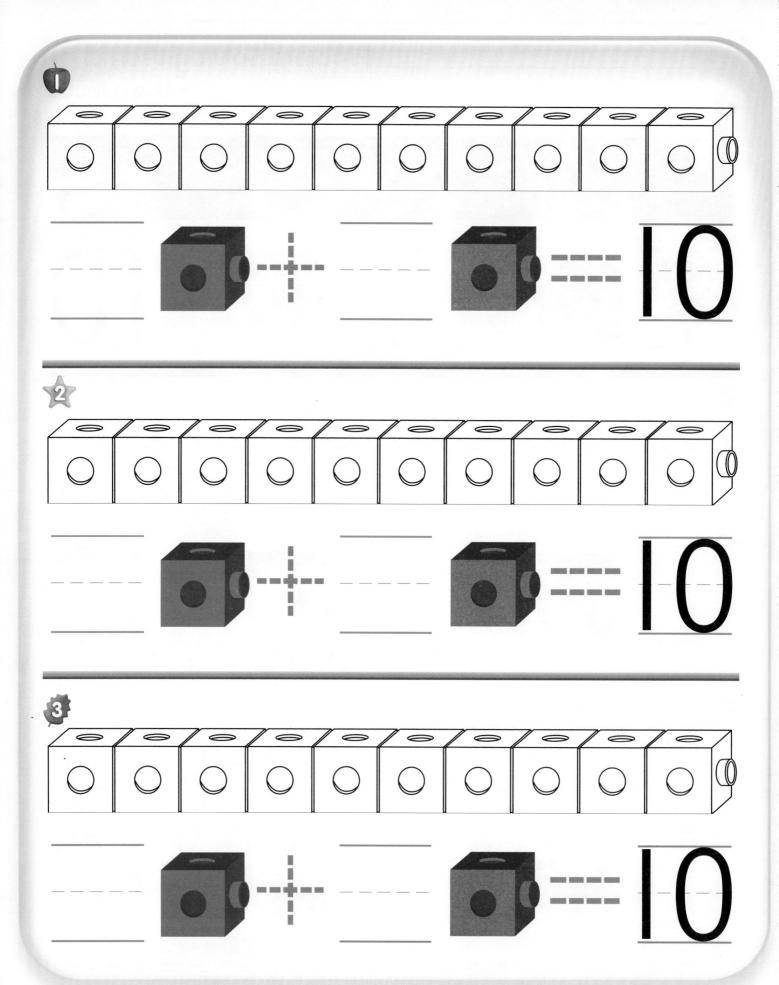

**DIRECTIONS** 1–3. Use two colors of cubes to model different ways to make 10. Color the cubes. Complete the addition sentence for each model.

 **HOME ACTIVITY** • Give your child ten pennies. Have your child arrange the coins to show different combinations of heads and tails. Write the addition sentences.

**312** three hundred twelve

# PRACTICE GAME Spin to Add

### Spin to Add

| | |
|---|---|
| **Player 1** | |
| **Player 2** | |

**DIRECTIONS** Play with a partner. Decide who goes first. Take turns spinning to get a number from each spinner. Use cubes to model your numbers and make a cube train to show how many in all. Compare your cube train with your partner's. Make a tally mark on the table for the player who has more cubes. The player who has the most tally marks after five spins wins the game.

**MATERIALS** two paper clips, pencils, connecting cubes

# Math Power • Doubles and Near Doubles

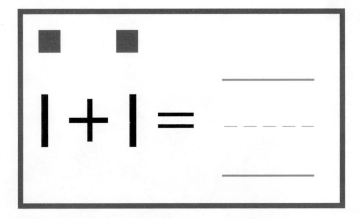

$1 + 1 =$ _____

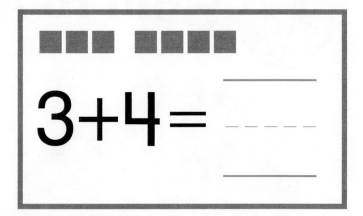

$3+4=$ _____

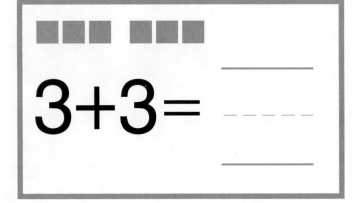

$3+3=$ _____

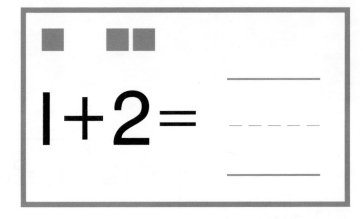

$2+3=$ _____

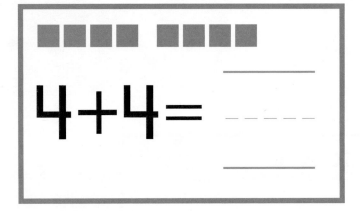

$4+4=$ _____

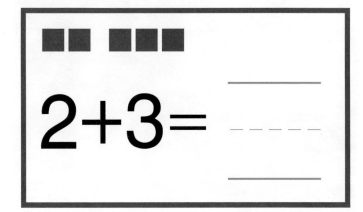

$1+2=$ _____

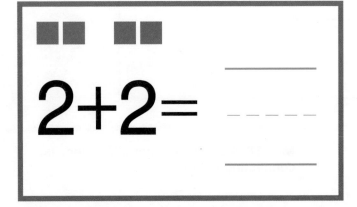

$2+2=$ _____

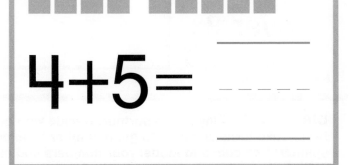

$4+5=$ _____

**DIRECTIONS** Complete the addition sentences for each model. Draw a line to the addition sentence that shows one more.

## ✓ Chapter 11 Review/Test

**1**

$$7 \quad + \quad 1 \quad = \quad \underline{\qquad}$$

**2**

$$\underline{\qquad} \quad + \quad \underline{\qquad} \quad = \quad \underline{\qquad}$$

**3**

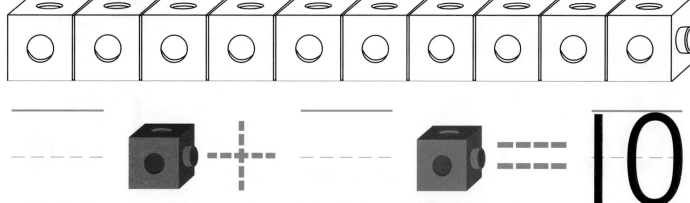

$$\underline{\qquad} \quad + \quad \quad = \quad 10$$

**DIRECTIONS** 1. How many shells? Draw one more shell. Write the number of shells in all to complete the addition sentence. 2. Tell a story about the objects. Complete the addition sentence. 3. Use two colors of cubes to show a way to make 10. Color the cubes. Complete the addition sentence.

# ✔ Cumulative Review

left 🖐        🖐 right

---

**2**

**before 7 o'clock**

**about 7 o'clock**

**after 7 o'clock**

---

**3**

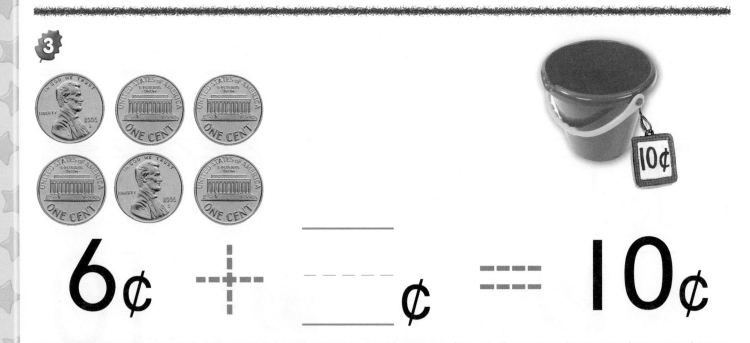

6¢ + ____¢ = 10¢

---

**DIRECTIONS**  **1.** Find the first object in the row, and hold it in your left hand. Find the rest of the objects in the row, and take turns holding each object in your right hand. Circle the object that is heavier than the object in your left hand.
**2.** Circle the time shown on the clock.  **3.** Use pennies to find the missing number. Draw the pennies. Write the missing number.

# CHAPTER 12 Subtraction
## Theme: Ocean Life

Name _____

**1**

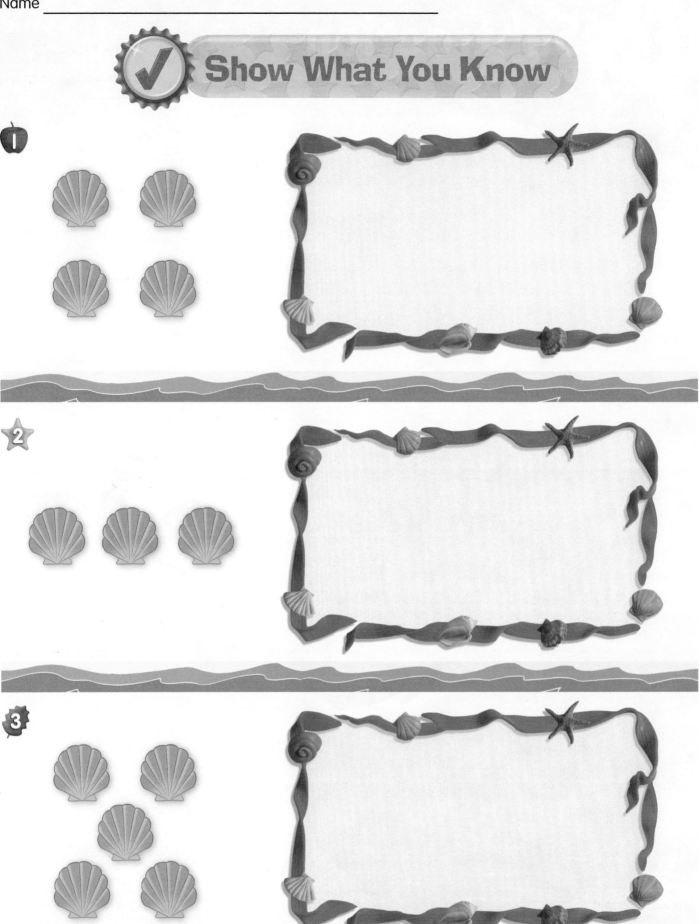

**2**

**3**

**DIRECTIONS**   1–3. How many shells? Draw a set with one fewer shell.

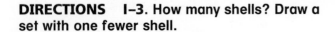 **Family Note:** This page checks your child's understanding of important concepts and skills needed for success in Chapter 12.

© Harcourt

# Problem Solving Workshop

## Strategy • Act It Out

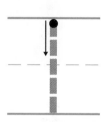

**DIRECTIONS** **1–2.** Listen to and act out the story. Write the number that shows how many children are left.

**OBJECTIVE** • Solve problems by using the strategy *act it out*.

**DIRECTIONS** **1.** Listen to and act out the story. Write the number that shows how many books are left. **2.** Listen to and act out the story. Write the number that shows how many cups are left.

 **HOME ACTIVITY ·** Tell your child a short subtraction story. Have your child use toys to act out the story and then write the number that shows how many toys are left.

**320** three hundred twenty

**Model Subtraction**

3     1     2

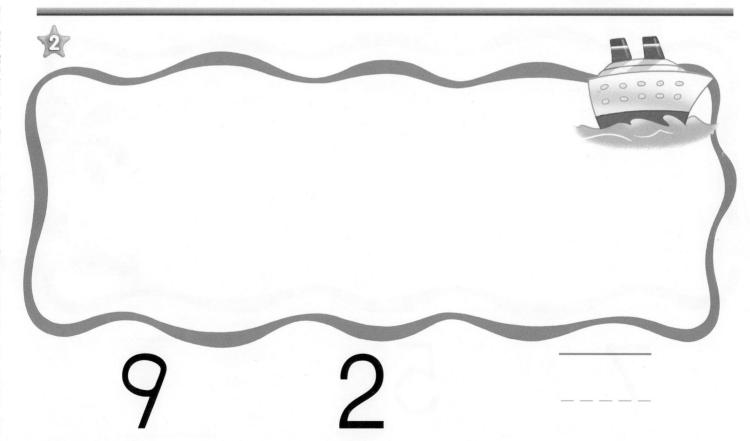

9     2     _____

**DIRECTIONS** 1–2. Listen to the story. Model the story with cubes. Write the number that shows how many are left.

**OBJECTIVE** • Use concrete objects to model subtraction.

**1**

4          3          _____

**2**

7          5          _____

**DIRECTIONS** 1–2. Listen to the story. Model the story with cubes. Write the number that shows how many are left.

 **HOME ACTIVITY** • Tell your child a short subtraction story. Have your child act out the story using objects and tell how many objects are left.

© Harcourt

**1**

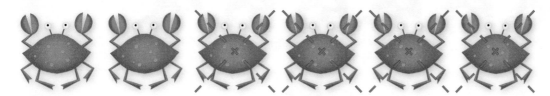

 take away **4** is

**2**

_____ take away **7** is _____

**3**

_____ take away **5** is _____

**DIRECTIONS   1–3.** Write how many there are in all. Mark an X on the animals that are taken away. Write how many are left.

**OBJECTIVE** • Use pictures to understand separating groups.

**1**

_____ _____

_____ take away **4** is _____

**2**

_____ _____

_____ take away **2** is _____

**3**

_____ _____

_____ take away **7** is _____

**DIRECTIONS  1–3.** Write how many there are in all. Mark an X on the animals that are taken away. Write how many are left.

 **HOME ACTIVITY ·** Have your child draw a group of ten or fewer balloons and then mark an X on some balloons to show that they have popped. Have your child write the number that tells how many balloons are left.

**1**

| 7 | take away | 4 | is | 3 |
|---|---|---|---|---|

**2**

| 10 | take away | 6 | is | 4 |
|---|---|---|---|---|

**3**

| 8 | take away | 2 | is | 6 |
|---|---|---|---|---|

**DIRECTIONS  1–3.** Write how many fish there are in all. Mark an X on the fish that are taken away. Complete the subtraction sentence to show how many are left.

OBJECTIVE • Use symbols to represent subtraction sentences.

© Harcourt

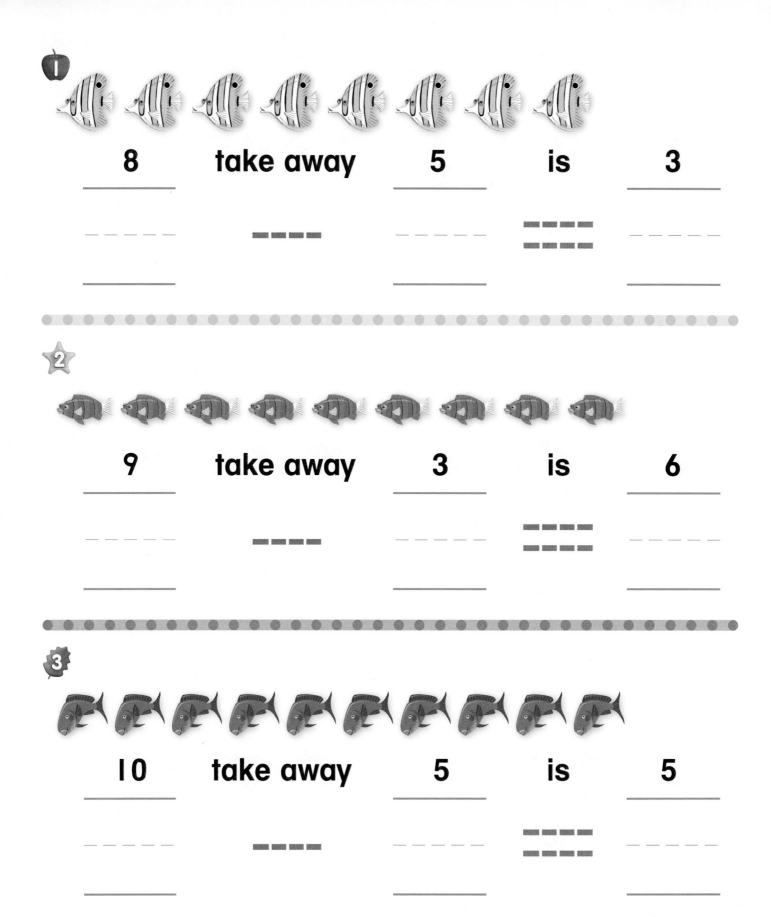

**1**

8     take away     5     is     3

**2**

9     take away     3     is     6

**3**

10     take away     5     is     5

**DIRECTIONS** 1–3. Write how many fish there are in all. Mark an X on the fish that are taken away. Complete the subtraction sentence to show how many are left.

 **HOME ACTIVITY** • Ask your child to choose one subtraction sentence on the page. Have your child point to the sign used to represent *take away* and the sign that shows *is equal to*. Ask your child to tell you which number shows how many in all, which shows how many are being taken away, and which shows how many are left.

# ✓ Mid Chapter 12 Review

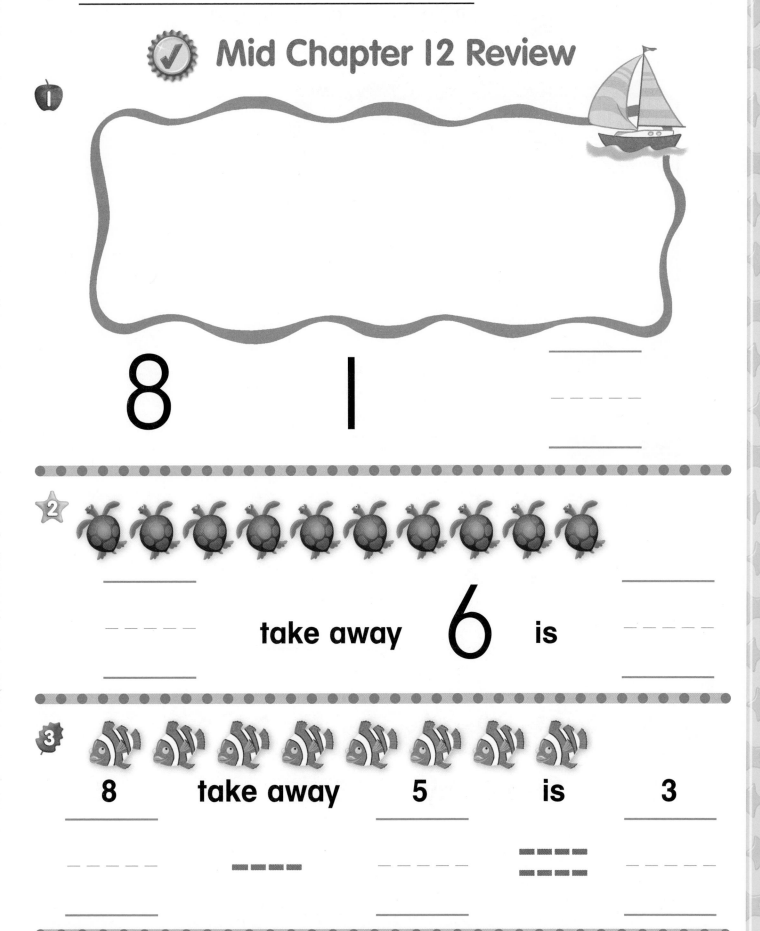

8    1    _____

2    _____ take away **6** is _____

_____

3    8    take away    5    is    3

_____    ----    _____    ====
====
_____

**DIRECTIONS** 1. Listen to the story. Model the story with cubes. Write the number that shows how many are left. 2. Write chow many there are in all. Mark an X on the animals that are taken away. Write how many are left. 3. Write how many fish there are in all. Mark an X on the fish that are taken away. Complete the subtraction sentence to show how many are left.

# ✔ Cumulative Review

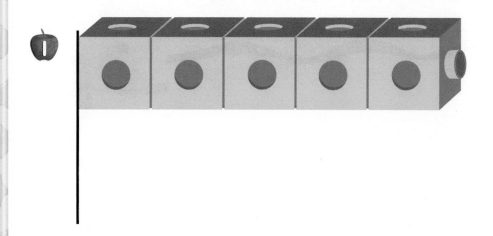

---

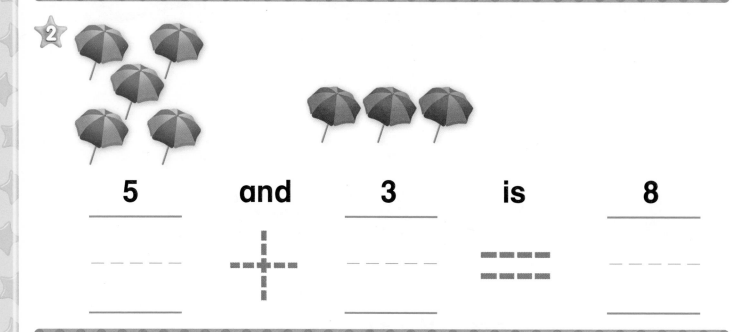

| 5 | and | 3 | is | 8 |
|---|---|---|---|---|
| _____ | + | _____ | = | _____ |

---

10    take away    5    is    5

_____    ----    _____    =    _____

_____

---

**DIRECTIONS** **1.** Make a cube train that is the same length. Draw the cube train. **2.** Write how many in each group. Circle the two groups. Trace the symbols. Write how many in all. **3.** Write how many fish there are in all. Mark an X on the fish that are taken away. Complete the subtraction sentence to show how many are left.

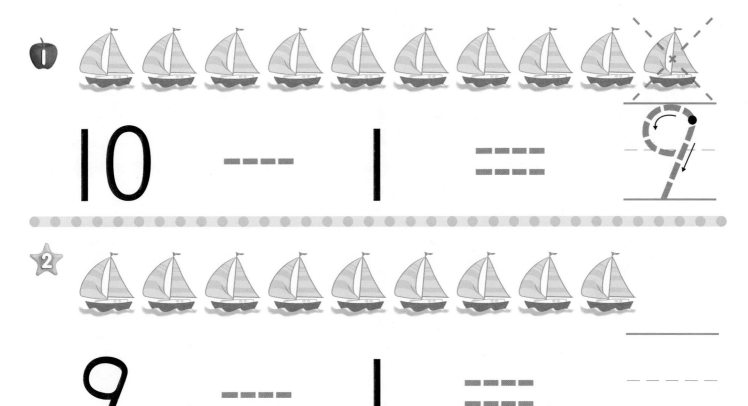

🍎 **1**

$$10 - 1 = 9$$

⭐ **2**

$$9 - 1 = \underline{\hspace{2cm}}$$

🍂 **3**

$$8 - 1 = \underline{\hspace{2cm}}$$

🌼 **4**

$$7 - 1 = \underline{\hspace{2cm}}$$

**DIRECTIONS 1–4.** How many boats are there in all? Mark an X on the boat that is taken away. Complete the subtraction sentence to show how many boats are left.

OBJECTIVE • Represent a number pattern of one less in subtraction sentences.

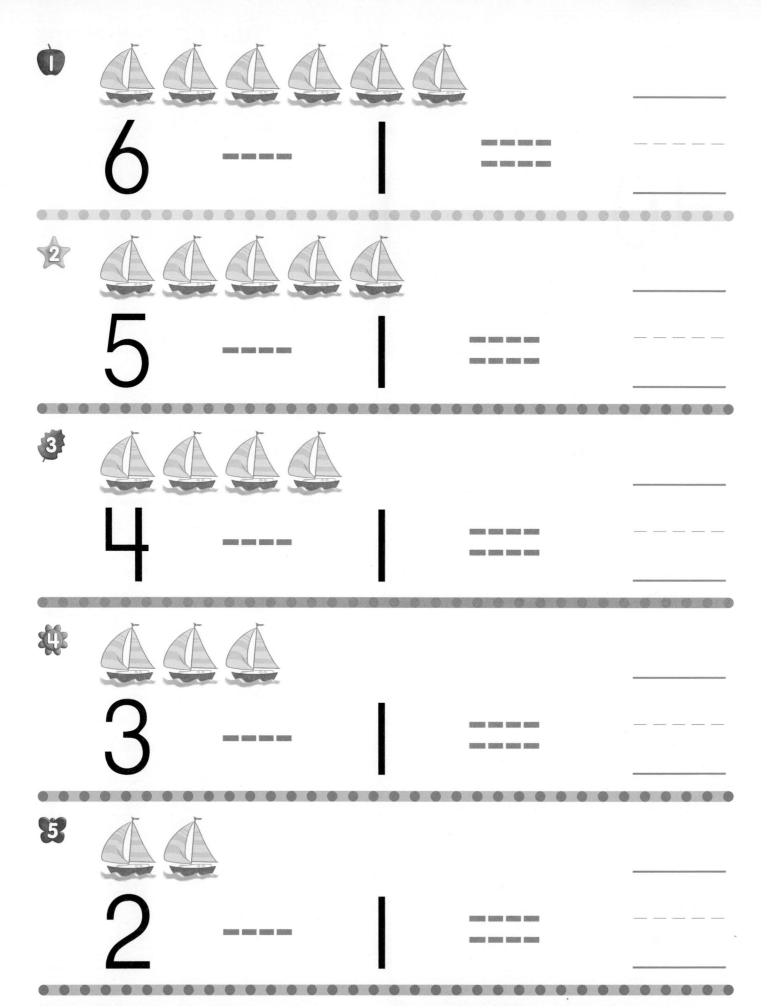

**1.**

$$6 - 1 = \underline{\hspace{2cm}}$$

**2.**

$$5 - 1 = \underline{\hspace{2cm}}$$

**3.**

$$4 - 1 = \underline{\hspace{2cm}}$$

**4.**

$$3 - 1 = \underline{\hspace{2cm}}$$

**5.**

$$2 - 1 = \underline{\hspace{2cm}}$$

**DIRECTIONS** 1–5. How many boats are there in all? Mark an X on the boat that is taken away. Complete the subtraction sentence to show how many boats are left.

 **HOME ACTIVITY** · Ask your child to use toys to demonstrate and describe the number pattern shown on this page.

Name _____

# Subtraction Sentences

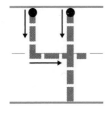    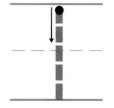

4 − 3 = 1

____ − ____ = ____

____ − ____ = ____

**DIRECTIONS  1–3.** Tell a story about the birds. Complete the subtraction sentence.

OBJECTIVE • Complete simple subtraction sentences.

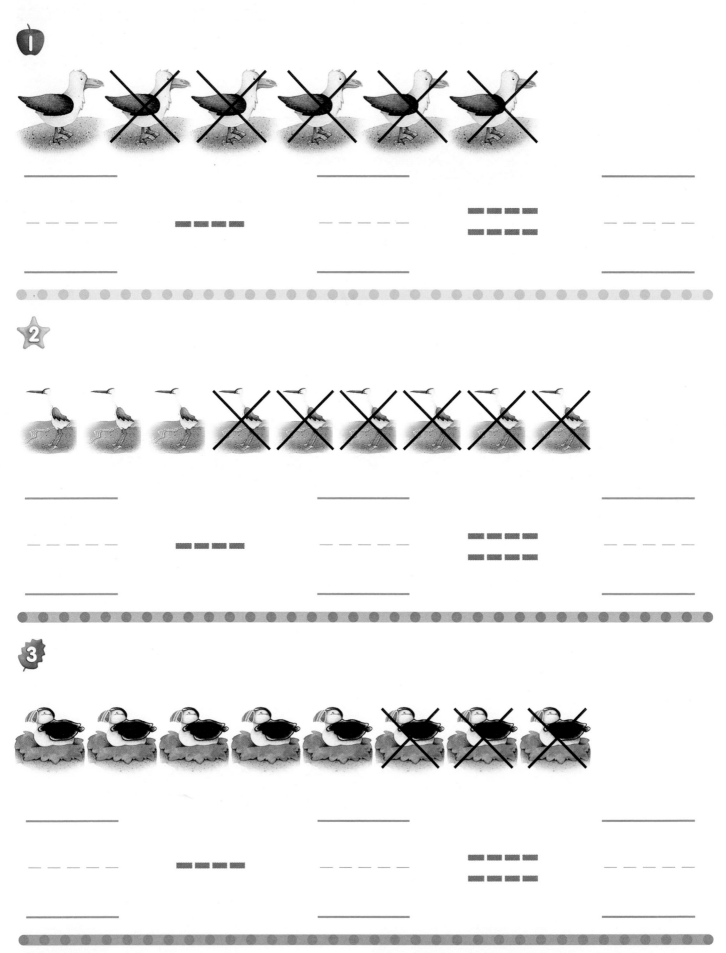

**DIRECTIONS** 1–3. Tell a story about the birds. Complete the subtraction sentence.

 **HOME ACTIVITY** • Give your child some books, and then take some away. Ask your child to tell a subtraction story about the books. Then write these symbols and have your child complete the subtraction sentence: __ – __ = __.

**332** three hundred thirty-two

Name _____

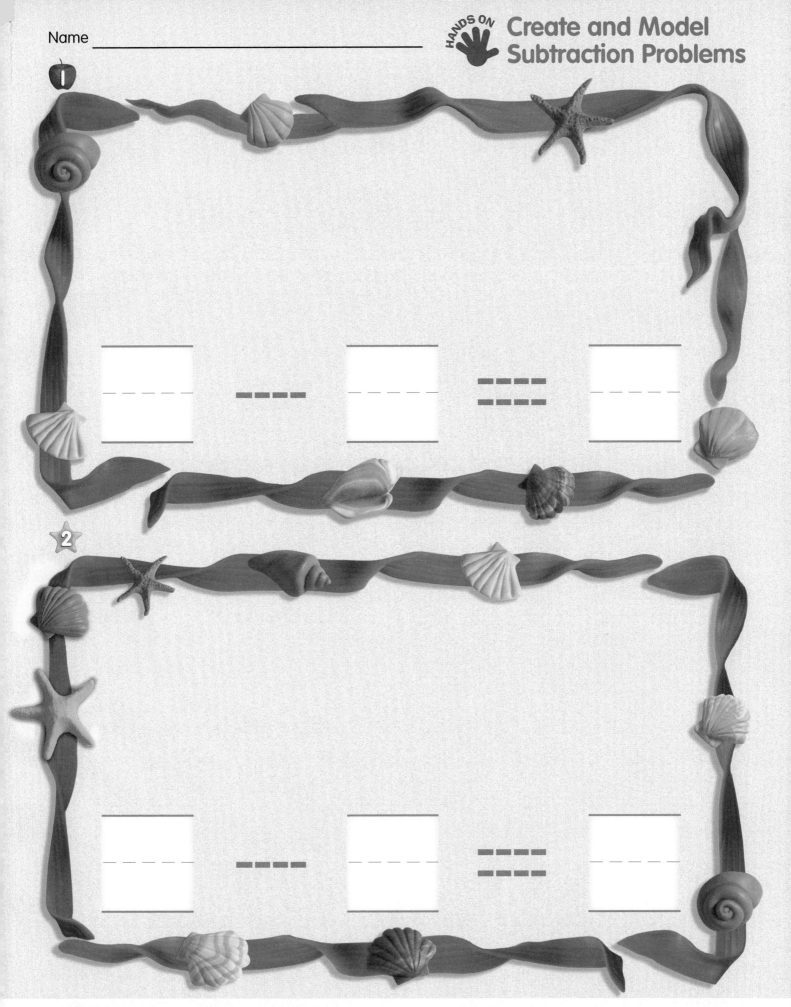

**Create and Model Subtraction Problems**

**1**

$$ \boxed{\phantom{XXX}} - \boxed{\phantom{XXX}} = \boxed{\phantom{XXX}} $$

**2**

$$ \boxed{\phantom{XXX}} - \boxed{\phantom{XXX}} = \boxed{\phantom{XXX}} $$

**DIRECTIONS** 1–2. Tell a subtraction story. Model your story with counters. Draw the counters. Mark an X on the counters that are taken away. Complete the subtraction sentence.

**OBJECTIVE** • Use concrete objects to create and model a subtraction problem.

**Chapter 12 • Lesson 7**

three hundred thirty-three **333**

**1**

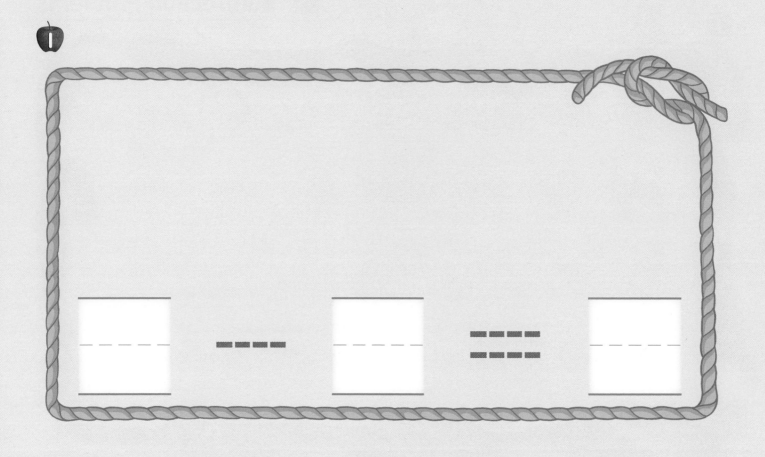

**2**

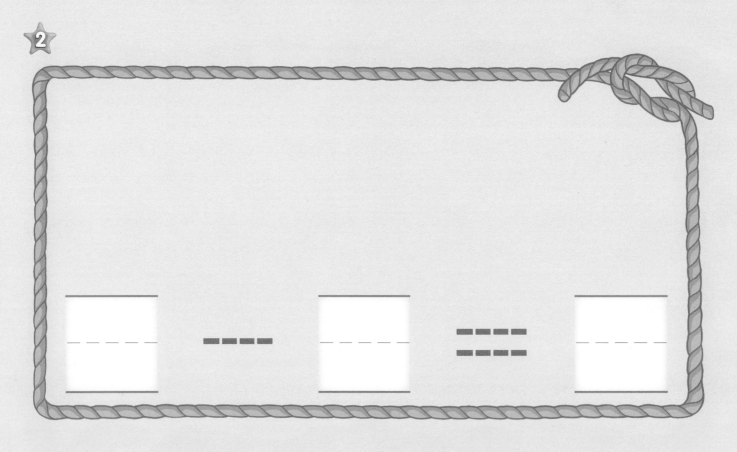

**DIRECTIONS  1–2. Tell a subtraction story. Model your story with counters. Draw the counters. Mark an X on the counters that are taken away. Complete the addition sentence.**

**HOME ACTIVITY** · Ask your child to choose one problem on the page. Have him or her tell you the subtraction story, and then explain the subtraction sentence.

**334** three hundred thirty-four

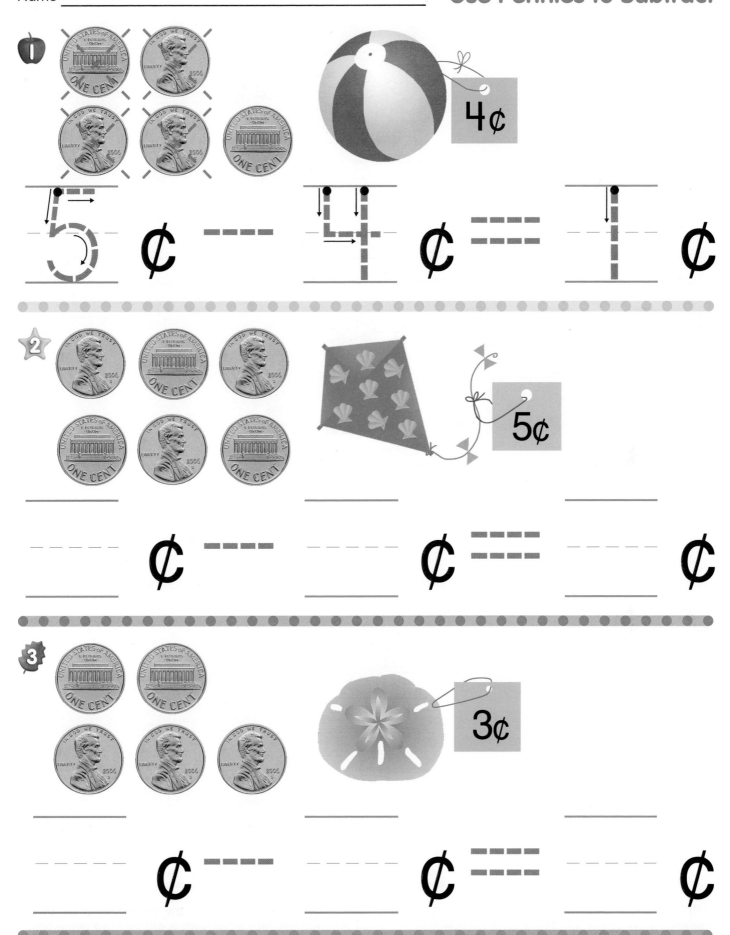

**DIRECTIONS** 1–3. Write how many pennies there are in all. Mark an X on the number of pennies it would take to buy the toy. Write that number. Then complete the subtraction sentence.

OBJECTIVE • Use pennies to solve subtraction problems.

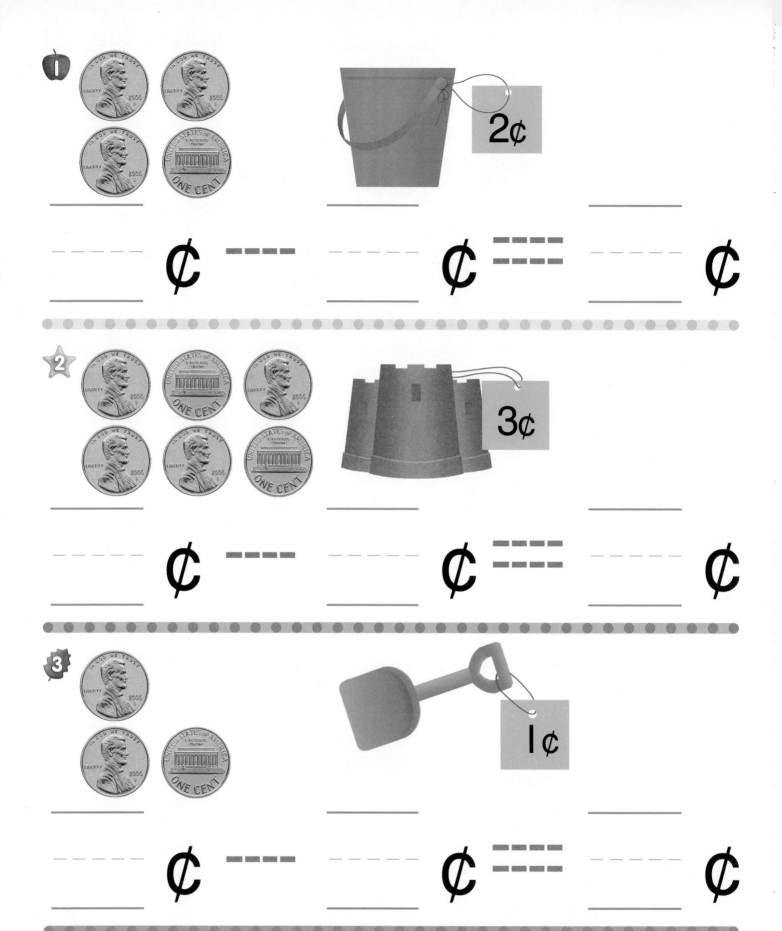

_____ ¢ – – – – – _____ ¢ ≡≡≡ _____ ¢

_____ ¢ – – – – – _____ ¢ ≡≡≡ _____ ¢

_____ ¢ – – – – – _____ ¢ ≡≡≡ _____ ¢

**DIRECTIONS** **1–3.** Write how many pennies there are in all. Mark an X on the number of pennies it would take to buy the toy. Write that number. Then complete the subtraction sentence.

 **HOME ACTIVITY** • Show your child a set of 8 pennies and a toy with a sticky-note price tag of 5¢. Write the following symbols: __¢ – __¢ = __¢. Have your child complete the subtractioin sentence to show what would happen if he or she bought the toy with the money. Repeat with other groups of up to 10 pennies and with toys priced from 1¢ to 9¢.

© Harcourt

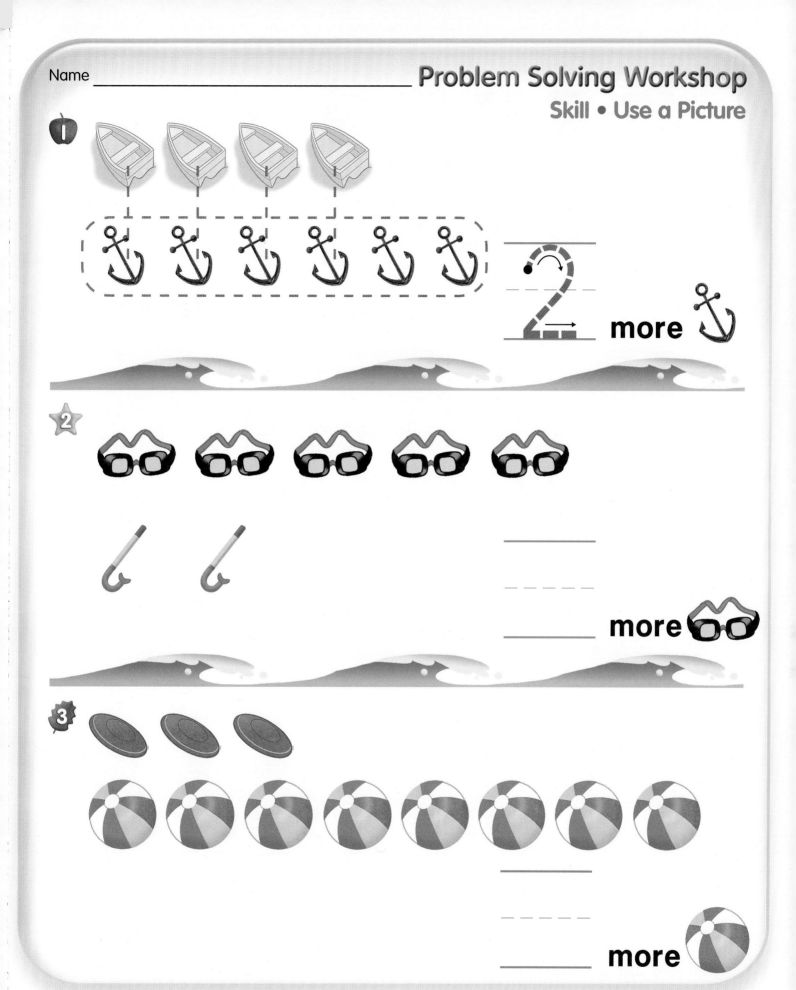

**1** 2 more ⚓

**2** _____
_____ more 👓

**3** _____
_____ more 🏖

**DIRECTIONS** 1–3. Draw lines to match the objects in the top row to the objects in the bottom row. Compare the groups. Circle the group that has more objects, and write how many more.

**OBJECTIVE •** Solve problems by using the skill *use a picture*.

© Harcourt

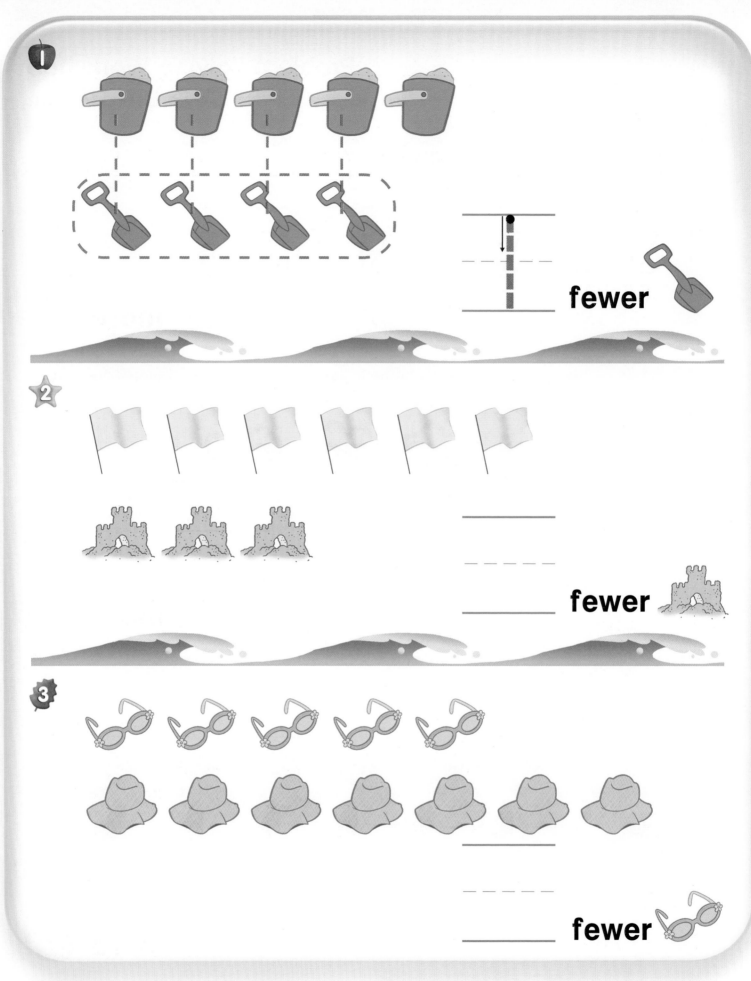

**1**

**fewer**

**2**

_____

- - - - - -

_____ **fewer**

**3**

_____

- - - - - -

_____ **fewer**

**DIRECTIONS** **1–3.** Draw lines to match the objects in the top row to the objects in the bottom row. Compare the groups. Circle the group that has fewer objects, and write how many fewer.

**HOME ACTIVITY** · Show your child a row of 7 pennies and a row of 3 nickels. Have your child compare the groups, identify which has fewer coins, and tell how many fewer. Repeat with other groups of coins up to ten.

**338** three hundred thirty-eight

© Harcourt

Name _____

# Sailboat Subtraction

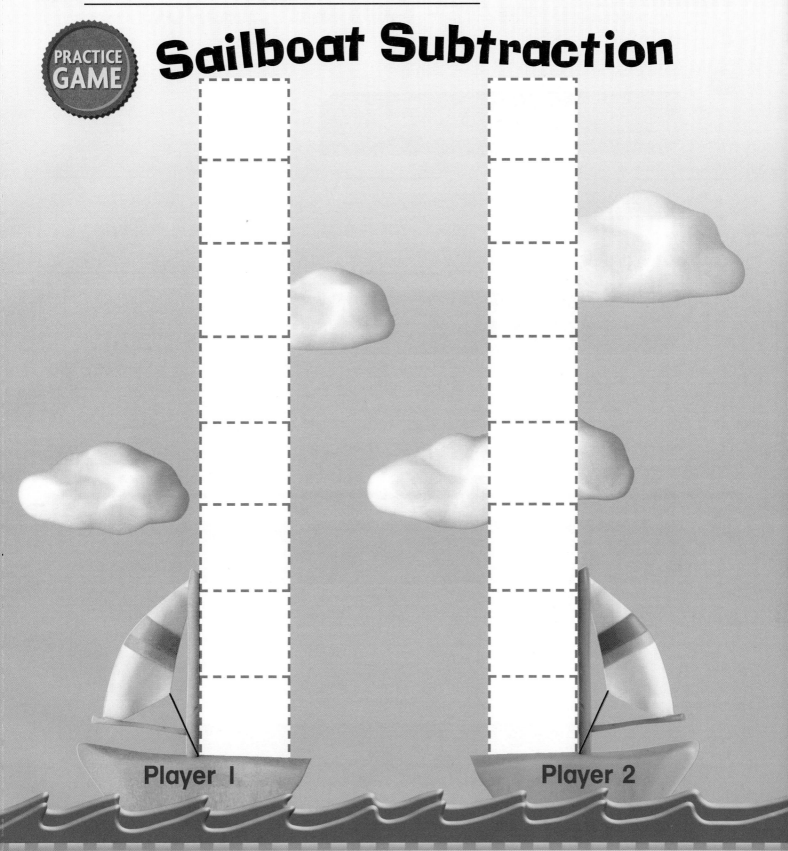

**Player 1**

**Player 2**

**DIRECTIONS** Play with a partner. Each player starts with an 8-cube train on the workspace. Decide who goes first. Take turns rolling the number cube. Subtract the number of cubes shown on the number cube. After each roll, tell your number sentence. If the number rolled is more than the cubes you have left, you must add that many cubes. The player who subtracts all their cubes wins the game.

**MATERIALS** number cube (1-3); 8 connecting cubes for each player

# Math Power • Add and Subtract

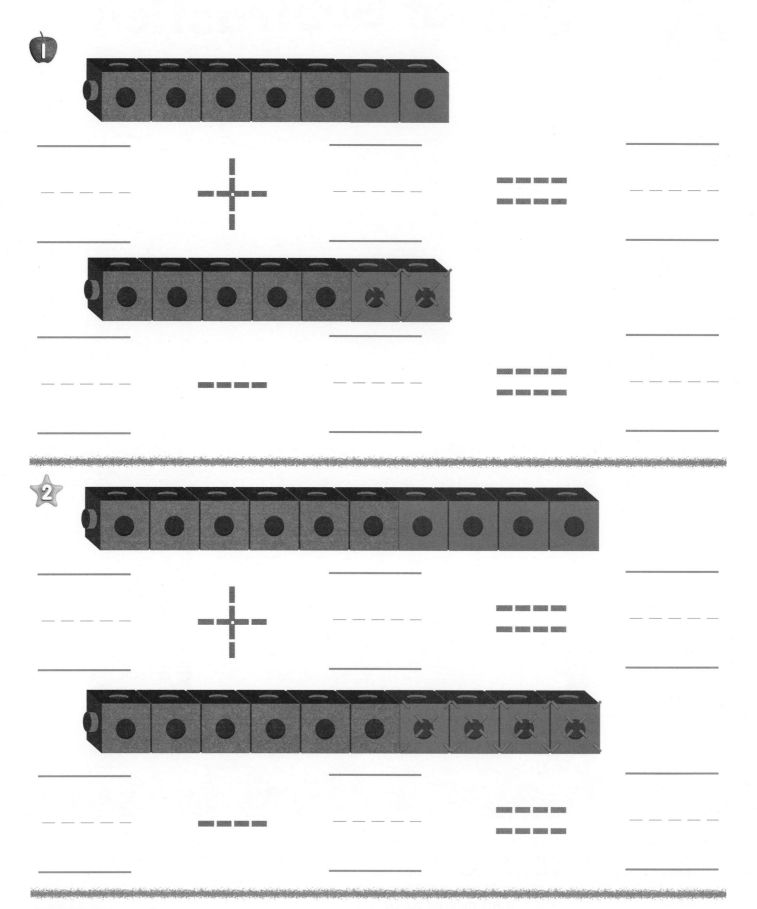

**DIRECTIONS**   **1-2.** Use cubes to add and to subtract. Complete the sentences.

## ✓ Chapter 12 Review/Test

**1**

5 --- 1 === _____

**2**

**3**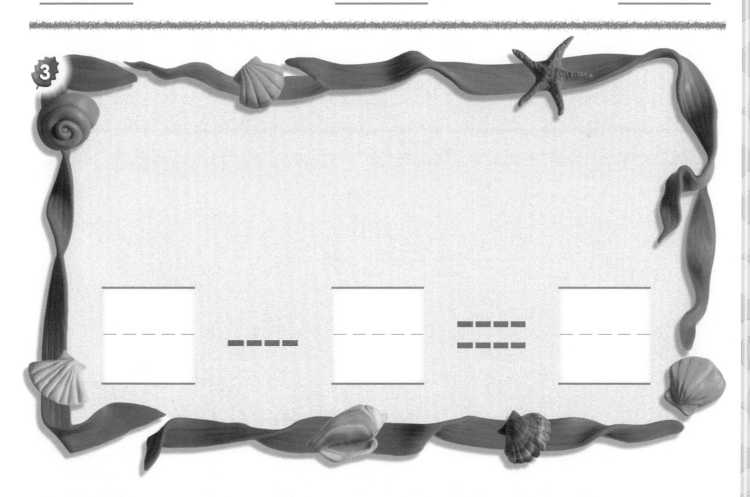

**DIRECTIONS** **1.** How many boats are there in all? Mark an X on the boat that is taken away. Complete the subtraction sentence to show how many boats are left. **2.** Tell a story about the birds. Complete the subtraction sentence. **3.** Tell a subtraction story. Model your story with counters. Draw the counters. Mark an X on the counters that are taken away. Complete the subtraction sentence.

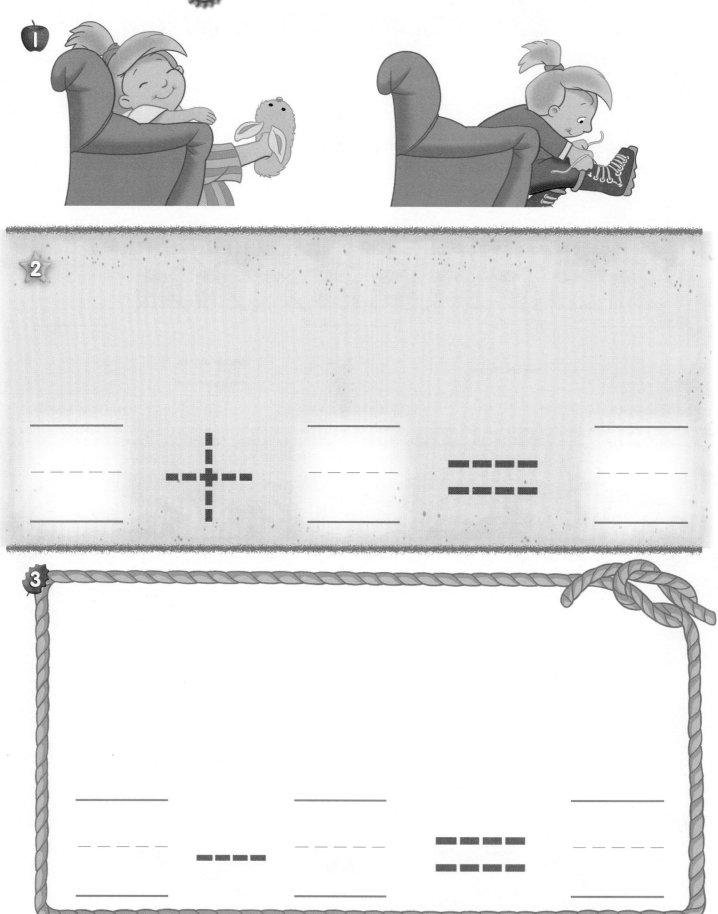

**DIRECTIONS** **I.** Circle the activity that usually takes more time. **2.** Tell an addition story. Model your story with counters. Draw the counters. Use count on to find the sum. Complete the addition sentence. **3.** Tell a subtraction story. Model your story with counters. Draw the counters. Mark an X on the counters that are taken away. Complete the subtraction sentence.

**342** three hundred forty-two

# THE WORLD ALMANAC FOR KIDS
## Colorful Coral

**ALMANAC Fact**

Coral is not a plant or a rock. It is a tiny animal called a coral polyp.

Problem Solving

1 _____ + _____ = _____

2 _____ + _____ = _____

**DIRECTIONS** 1. Tell an addition story about the red corals in the picture. Complete the addition sentence. 2. Tell an addition story about the purple corals in the picture. Complete the addition sentence.

 **TALK Math** Tell other addition stories about the corals you see on the page.

# Fishy Subtraction

**1**

_____  **—**  _____  **=**  _____

**2**

_____  **—**  _____  **=**  _____

**DIRECTIONS**  **1.** How many fish are there in all? Mark an X on the fish swimming away. Complete the subtraction sentence.  **2.** Draw your own school of fish. Draw some fish swimming away. Mark an X on those fish. Then complete the subtraction sentence.

 Explain your fish story.

© Harcourt

# Workmat 1

workmat 1 (sorting mat)

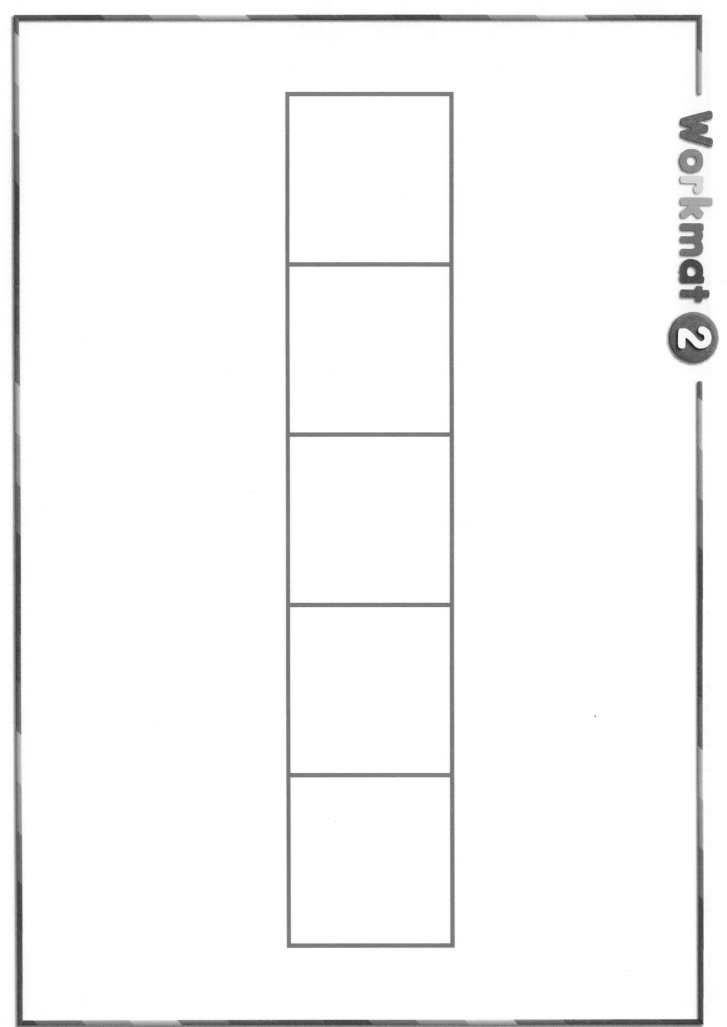

**346** three hundred forty-six

workmat 2 (five frame)

© Harcourt

**Workmat 3**

# Workmat 4

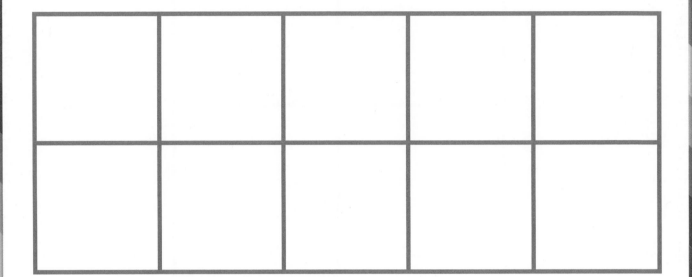

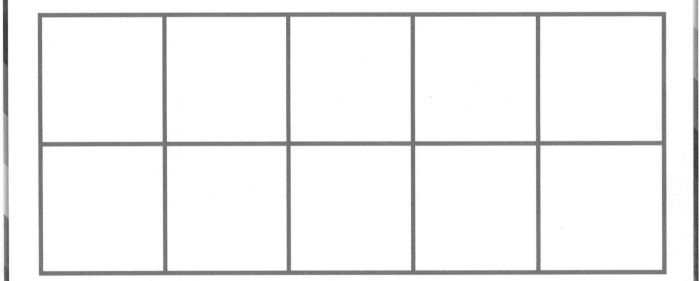

workmat 4 (ten frames)

# Photo Credits

**Page Placement Key:** (t) top, (b) bottom, (c) center, (l) left, (r) right, (bg) background, (i) insert.

**Front Cover:** (l) ImageState/Alamy; (r) Philip Lee Harvey/Getty Images.

**Back Cover:** (l) Philip Lee Harvey/Getty Images; (r) Juniors Bildarchiv/Alamy.

**Table of Contents**
iv-xii Jeff Rotman/Getty Images.

**UNIT 1**
**Chapter 1**
3 Laurence Mouton/PhotoAlto/Jupiterimages; 20 (bl) Mihaela Ninic/Alamy; 21 (b) Losevsky Pavel/Shutterstock RF; 28 (br) Scott Rothstein/Shutterstock.

**Chapter 2**
56 (tc) C Squared Studios/Getty Images; (tr) Grant Heilman/Grant Heilman Photography.

**UNIT 2**
**Storybook**
F (t) blickwinkel / Alamy; (t) Digital Archive Japan/Alamy; (t) Eureka/Alamy; (t) Poprugin Aleksey/Shutterstock; H (tl) Chris Turner/Shutterstock; (tr) Jan Kopec/Getty; (bl) Terrance Klassen/Alamy; (br) Darrell Gulin/CORBIS.

**Chapter 3**
59 Photodisc Royalty Free/Fotosearch.

**Chapter 4**
89 Johnathan Smith; Cordaiy Photo Library Ltd./CORBIS; 101 (tl) Dirk Anschutz/ Getty Images; (cl) Getty Images RF; (bl) Juniors Bildarchiv/Alamy; 102 (bl) D. Hurst/Alamy; 114 (t) Shutterstock; (b) Shutterstock; 117 (tr) Inga Spence/Visuals Unlimited; 118 (bg) Paul Taylor/Getty Images; B (cr) Federico Gambarini/dpa/Corbis; C (tl) Jan Kopec/Getty; (c) Chris Turner/Shutterstock; D (t) Darrell Gulin/CORBIS; (cr & b) Terrance Klassen/Alamy; E (tl) Randall Ingalls/Alamy; (tc) Peter Arnold, Inc./Alamy; (cr) Mira.

**UNIT 3**
**Storybook**
E (c) Olga Lyubkina/Shutterstock; G (tl) Shutterstock; H (t) Olga Lyubkina/Shutterstock.

**Chapter 5**
121 Johnny Johnson/Getty Images

**Chapter 6**
145 Jeff Rotman/Getty Images; 147 (tr) D. Hurst/Alamy; (bc) D. Hurst / Alamy; (c) PhotoDisc, Inc / Harcourt; (b) ShutterStock RF; (cr) Stephen Coburn/Shutterstock; 150 (tl) Ingvald Kaldhussater/Shutterstock; 152 (bl) Harcourt Telescope; 154 (cl) Mehmet Alci/Shutterstock RF; (c) Patsy A. Jacks/Shutterstock RF; 159 (tr) Stephen Coburn/Shutterstock; 164 (tr) Foodfolio/Alamy Images; 171 (cl) Foodfolio/Alamy Images; 173 (tc) GK Hart/Vikki Hart/Getty Images; (tr) Steven Burr Williams/Getty Images.

**UNIT 4**
**Chapter 7**
177 Ariel Skelley/CORBIS; 180 (bg) Rosemary Calvert/Gettyimages; 182 (inset) Martin Ruegner/Gettyimages; 183 (c) Elena Elisseeva/Shutterstock RF; (b) Elena Elisseeva/Shutterstock RF; 184 (bg) Schnare & Stief/gettyimages.

**Chapter 8**
228 (r) Bill Smith Studio

**UNIT 5**
**Chapter 9**
231 Dorit Lombroso Photography; 240 Borut Gorenjak/Shutterstock; 242 (b) Borut Gorenjak/Shutterstock; 248 (c) Michael Thompson/Shutterstock RF.

**Chapter 10**
259 Royalty-Free/Corbis; 286 (cr) Michael Thompson/Shutterstock RF; 288 (r) Getty Images.

**UNIT 6**
**Chapter 11**
291 Getty Images RF.

**Chapter 12**
317 Randy Wells/Corbis; 343 (t) Jupiterimages; 344 (r) Getty/Harcourt.

All other photos © Harcourt School Publishers. Harcourt Photos provided by the Harcourt Index, Harcourt IPR, and Harcourt photographers; Weronica Ankarorn, Eric Camden, Don, Couch, Doug Dukane, Ken Kinzie, April Riehm, and Steve Williams.